D0713552

RITES OF THE DRAGON™

RITES OF THE DRAGON ™

TABLE OF CONTENTS

PROLOGUE: UNDER UNCERTAIN STARS

Were I a pagan bard, I would invoke a muse of fire to fill me with passion for the task ahead. I would beg a god to put his words in me, to blow his wisdom through me like a trumpet, to make me resound with truth for the people.

I am no pagan bard. My enemy is fire, and I am more likely to rebuke my passions than to bid them spill forth.

What am I? I have been a tyrant, a warrior, and one of the fallen on battle's field. I have been a Christian and a wanderer and an enemy of God. I have begged and murdered, tortured and rescued, pledged loyalty and given treachery.

I have died and returned and I drink hot blood.

My name is Vladislaus, onetime Prince of Wallachia, onetime commander of armies. Called Tepes, called Kaziglu Bey, called Dracula, I am now much more than once I was. Perhaps much less, as well.

I write this in Rome, far from my ancestral seat, far from my adopted home. Here I rest, sated by my beloved as she hunts on my behalf, luring men to their doom upon my table. Men only, for she is a jealous creature. She believes I have sent the others away for love of her, and that is the truth. It is not, however, the entire truth.

I put them aside from fear. I fear their jealousy of her. I fear the fate of all I have dragged down into my doom. All things alter, as she knows as well as any. She fights against this change, foolishly, and her struggles may but speed it. I have learned, to my sorrow, that nothing I can do endures. She will be lost to me, and it is my damnation to choose if I lose her swiftly or by inches and decades, but inevitably she will slip my grasp.

How can she think she will remain, when all is flux and chaos? In Paris, in the icy North, in the heated East, the watchers of the sky are amazed, chapfallen, at the prodigy in Cassiopeia these recent years past. The holy aether, untouched and immutable, is now shown to be fickle as the love of man. A new star flares, unseen and uncharted— no bearded vagabond, like the shaggy star of 1456 which shone on my first, brief reign, but a fixed light! As if the angels of the spheres had untimely coupled, birthing a celestial bastard. If even the stately constant tread of stars is vulnerable to change, how can any earthly thing be fixed?

I study the heavens. I study the words of ancients. I study the signs I see, and those I taste in the flesh of those around me. I know the time draws near.

Soon I will sleep, and it is good that I will sleep. Too much strength is overpowering for us. My beloved weeps, she wipes her crimson tears with golden tresses, but I am not sad. Those around me fear the great slumber, shy away from the nightmares and visions, but not I. They see a prison, another torment, another cage forged by God for their worthless souls.

They are blind.

I see opportunity. I see a road before me, a new world to explore and conquer. The elders tell me in chastened tones about the madness of their resting visions, but I saw, beyond their fears—the loss of self, the loss of sense, the loss of memory—tools of surpassing potential, if only the hand that grasps them is strong.

I shall sleep but not rest. I gird myself for battle, not of the body, but of the mind. As I lie in torpor I shall duel my weaker selves, I shall kill any memory that makes me less than I ought to be, less than I need to be, less than the greatest of my kind.

The visions of the elders were oracular, though in their terror they kenned not what they saw. When I triumph in this new combat, this unseen and still place beyond reason and closed eyes, what wonders of knowledge will be my plunder?

Even now the
stillness creeps upon
me. Even now my bones are
weary, my muscles groan with the
stiffness that is their deathly due. Each day is a greater weight, every sleep harder
to batter back. Soon it will crush me, and like a young bride who yearns for the
harsh strength of her lover's arms, I shall revel in being crushed.

Before my slumber war, however, a task remains. Like any good scholar, I
must put my books in order.

It is typical of my kind to keep a book of memories, as if mere ink on paper
could contradict a Reason bent on torpor's lathe. My books have a different
purpose. They are no fruitless attempt to taste again air once breathed, to be
again the youth I was. No, their role is to trace the changes worked in, through
and upon me. I am not the angry and ignorant monster whose home was stolen.
I am not the sorrowing scholar who lurked in his ruin. I am not even the tem-
perate teacher who set forth to bring new knowledge. I am none of those things
but was all. I change, I am remade, I am both the sword and the smith who
forges it. Who is to say that I, as I am now, cannot learn from the brute, the
student, the prophet? Every season has its lesson, and every lesson has its price.
He is a fool indeed who scorns that which he has already bought at dear cost.

I turn my musty pages and recopy each word in my own hand. The temptation is there to change them—all things change, do they not? Is this not my credo? Yet I refrain. I will not sand away one bleat of self-pity, I will not soften any stark cruelty or brassy foolishness. Through changes without ceasing, something still and permanent can remain. I cannot see clearly ahead, but I can keep a grasp of what has gone before, even when my new self, new vision, sees through the shades that then held me blind.

This is my cause, my hope. That I can pierce the shadows of hate, and even the bright glister of love, and find beyond them something greater than either.

Let us end. Let us begin.

BOOK ONE:
THE BOOK OF THE DEAD

I rose up among the dead, and I was dead with them.

The Turks struck by night, damned infidels, coming in a horde like rats, and our gates were opened by a traitor within. We fought, my patriots and I, my bodyguard and I, two hundred men hand-picked by Prince Stephen the Great to defend my royal flesh, and yet it collapsed nonetheless on the thirsty ground.

My enemies paid for their triumph, paid dearly. For every stripe upon me I took a life, and for each of the fallen by my side, two arrayed against me perished. It was good war. It was cold, and mad with noise, and the stink of a man when his bowels are opened, it was all that I was born to do. An arrow struck my shield where it had splintered under a spear thrust, it glanced off upward and transfixed my lip and my nose, the pain was maddening and the blood poured down my throat. Every breath choked me and each shout sprayed crimson.

Then I saw him and I knew him. A thick brute who had curried my horse, grinned and bowed, now dressed in the armor of my enemy. I remembered no name for him but it must have been he who betrayed our position. I saw him and he saw me and we knew each other. In that moment death passed between us and we were married, tied together in hatred. Stronger than the ropes of seed that tie a woman to a man are the chains of blood that tie a warrior to his enemy. Six men, mixed of his and mine, stood between us, and then three, and then one. That last was my loyal friend, yet I shoved him aside, eager for my nemesis.

With no word spoken we locked arms, his pagan sword to my axe, and with cruel joy he shouldered the very arrow in my face, I fell back as he raised his weapon, but the pain had not felled me, the pain had made me fierce. I cut him through at the knee, at the join of his plates and bones, and he fell, but falling, struck. The blade sheared my side through, and now each breath was mixed with blood from above and below. He crashed upon me, face to face in the ardor of combat, he pinned my weapon so I clawed off his helmet and raked him like a cat while he turned his scimitar, ground it within me, like ice and fire shearing in my side. My other hand found his throat as his face eclipsed the moon, his nose and mouth bleeding into me— or was it my own blood, spat upon him, dripping back?—and even as I crushed his throat I felt the spirit in me slip free.

UBENSTEIN·4

In an instant all was still and clear. I rose up and the fierce cruelty of battle was replaced, transfigured, as if all I beheld was made of shimmering light. Crystal soldiers beneath me gave silent groans and died but I was above it all, higher still, and I came into the luminous presence of the Almighty.

SON OF WALLACHIA,

said the Lord unto me,

IS YOUR WORK FINISHED?

"Oh great Lord," I said to Him, "Return me to the world, that I may smite the unbelievers in Your holy name!"

ARE THEY NOT MY CHILDREN TOO?

"They have rejected your Son! They have turned their backs on salvation and deserve only the scourge and the fire!"

AS DID THE BEGGARS AND INDIGENT OF YOUR NATION, WHOM YOU LURED WITH KIND PROMISE AND THEN BURNED ALIVE?

"Christ said for the poor come unto him. If any who died were saved, did I not send them to His presence?"

YOU SWORE AN OATH TO ME, CHILD OF THE DRAGON. BEFORE THE ALTAR AT SNAGOV, YOU SWORE TO SHOW THE TRUTH OF CHRIST TO YOUR PEOPLE, IF ONLY YOU WERE PERMITTED YOUR THRONE.

"I have kept my promise!"

INDEED? IN MY SIGHT YOU HAVE TORTURED AND MURDERED AND DISGRACED THE SACRED HUMAN FORM, WHICH IS IN MY IMAGE.

"I did as You did to Your son! Is any man better than Christ? Do any deserve less than the hurts He suffered? Every cry and groan was a hymn to Your glory! All that I did, I did in defense of Christendom! Ought I have let the Turk take them instead, and show them the tender mercy of Islam? Ought I have left them in indolence, to laze and fatten, to plot and scheme against me?"

I THE LORD AM JUDGE OF THE WORLD!

"By divine right, I the Prince am judge of my people!"

AS YOU WISH. YOUR WILL SHALL BE YOUR CURSE, DRAGON KNIGHT.

Instantly, I felt myself gripped once more by the inclining of Earth, plunging toward the battle-field once again.

TAKE DOMINION OVER MORTAL FLESH, BUT SURVIVE ENSLAVED TO IT. TAKE COMMAND OF THE BEASTS, FOR YOU EXCEL THEM IN SAVAGERY. YOU, WHO WOULD BE MY EQUAL, METE OUT DEATH TO HUMANKIND. BUT KNOW THAT FOR YOUR ARROGANCE, I HAVE MADE YOU UNCLEAN IN MY SIGHT, AND THE TOUCH OF PURITY SHALL HENCE-FORTH DRIVE YOU OUT. RE-MAIN IN DARKNESS UNTIL YOU LEARN, OR ELSE PER-ISH IN YOUR IGNORANCE.

The light drained out as down I fell, and at the moment of deep-est dark I was myself again. I felt the pain of my face, my side, I felt the agony of the world once more and I screamed, I rose up and cried my rage and misery. A black cloud of carrion birds rose and worse than my side, worse than my mouth, was the thirst that burned in every member. My Rational Soul was unseated and in its place the Animal reigned. I fell upon the dead, lapping the dried blood from armor and weapons, cutting my tongue on dirk and spearhead in my eagerness for more. I fed upon Christian and Muslim alike, I plunged my fingers into the mud and sucked at the battle-gore that seeped to fill the holes.

When I returned to myself—what self? Myself as *ghul*, as monster, as carrion devil!—I howled again, but this time cursing as a man. I cried to the sky my hatred of God, who had thrust this woe upon me. I swore that as He had made me for His enemy, I would be the direst foe He had fought, a worse Lucifer, a greater Judas, a name to blacken the world and a tor-ment for all humanity.

First, however, I would avenge myself upon my slayers.

First the soldiers, then the generals, and perhaps in time the great Sultan Mehmed himself. He will rue the day he challenged a Prince of Wallachia! Beside the evils I intend for him, his own blasphemy will seem a hymn of praise, his sodomy a sacrament, and his cruelty the balm of Gilead.

Clutching my axe and an unbroken shield, I made for Snagov monastery—the abbot there was loyal to me. But before I had gone a mile I scented blood and followed its lure.

Creeping through the chill dawn, I spied the Ottoman camp, the very soldiers who had taken me and mine. Like a hound that spies the hare, I could not be restrained. I rose up, I charged on foot, howling. They started and two were struck motionless, unmanned by cowardice, but the other two kept their wits and fired. Arrows pierced my shield and my flesh, but the hurts were nothing next to the call within me, clotted and dead blood calling for fresh. The guards shrieked the alarm as I fell on them and I was sunk in a delirium of lust for them, they were delicious in my sight, the maddening aroma of their life sweet in my nose and each who crowded forward was a new temptation, a new delight, a new delicacy and I the glutton who would taste them all.

Battle is always a red rapture, but this surpassed in sweetness any berserk fit I felt in life. To bite and kill these lowly Ottoman infantrymen gave me nearly the spiritual joy I had felt killing the pretenders Dan III and Vladislav II, who dared cast lecherous eyes on my throne and claim they had taken my fair nation in adultery. As for the physical bliss! It was transcendent.

I was struck a dozen times, a hundred, but with each kill and taste of blood I knit my flesh anew. Death ought to have come to me twenty times that night, but instead I stole the lives of my slayers, becoming stronger with each sanguine draught. I fought my way to their tents and fires and they fell back. My shield was tattered and I dropped it in favor of a severed arm, that I might sip sweet blood from it as I battled. I would have slain every man of the camp, save for an unforeseen peril, the rising of the sun.

I felt an awful sting, I smelled the charring of my flesh as my enemies rallied, arraying themselves with bows, the cowards, but their feathered sticks were nothing beside the agony of the breaking day. Much as I longed for the slaughtering bliss, I could not drive myself at them, into the light. Mad in terror, I cried out for the sky to fall on me, for the earth to swallow me.

The earth obeyed.

LAUBENSTEIN·4

When I arose from the sheltering soil, the Turks had fled their campsite and the shelter of darkness again roofed the sky.

I felt the hunger within me but it was less. Greater was the pain of my burns, sores showing where only the faintest bite of sunlight had fallen.

Alone, I had time to regroup my thoughts. Clearly I was far superior to any mortal—as any fit enemy of God must be. Their blood would be my food, as in living days I fed on their toil. So be it. It is fitting that the greater should meet their needs on the necks of the less.

Is this my fate, then? To be a lash on humanity's back? It is a duty to which I am fit, for I swear my thirst could drain the world, if only I had time enough and the power.

Yet inside the monster is the man, and the man craves revenge. Without aid I cannot be more than a pest, a small nuisance in the hinterlands of my own nation. No, to oppose and offend the Lord in any meaningful way, I need my throne, for even my terrific hate cannot corrupt all the world unaided.

To truly punish the Most High, I should pervert and corrupt that which is best in the world: The Christian Church. Yet while my hate is fierce for the Catholics who despised me in life, and the Christian rulers who betrayed me, like Matthias Corvinus and his father Hunyadi before him, that is nothing beside my loathing for the Turks. They who imprisoned me when only a child, who harassed me, who humiliated me with their threats and demands for tribute. Now Mehmet moves to put his catamite Radu upon my rightful throne, and that I will not stand. Even though it serves God's purpose for the nonce, I must slay the great Turk. Yes. I shall start my career of evil with the Ottomans. First I reclaim my throne from them, then I slay the Sultan, and then I negotiate with the new Sultan from a position of strength. For whose strength is greater than one who can hide in any patch of soil, who can refresh himself from any man or beast indefinitely, for whom common blood is the sovereign salve of any injury?

Before I could claim my kingdom, and then the world, I had first to reclaim a fortress. I turned my footsteps toward Snagov monastery, hoping to gather loyal troops on the way. To my shock and disgust, it soon became apparent that the triumph of my enemies was nearly complete. I saw few forces I could approach and demand fealty—my loyal soldiers had all perished by my side, Corvinus' Hungarians had abandoned me, and the fickle mercenaries in my employ had fled like dogs to lick a new master's heels.

I did encounter one small group of my secret police, but when I revealed myself they fled in terror, having heard accounts of my death. I gave them something to fear, in truth! Half who broke were run down before their companions, and I slaked my thirst upon their cowardly blood before the eyes of those stern enough to stand and fight. Once more I reminded them of their oaths to me, and having seen the might I now possess, they reconsidered their earlier flight.

With that paltry honor guard, I came at last to Snagov and demanded admittance as their rightful lord. The monks who rowed me across to their island fastness were pale and they trembled, perhaps more than they had even when I was their dread sovereign.

I took myself to the chapel to consult my friend the abbot, and there a dreadful thing befell me. As I opened the door and looked upon the holy ikon, a weakness filled my limbs and I was flung back. The abbot saw me fall and, thinking me wounded in body, ran to my side. Then he realized my wounds were altogether more grievous, and he stood back.

"My lord," he asked. "What has happened to you?"

"God has flung me from death to life. In battle I fell but, like Christ himself, I have returned!"

"No, my Prince. Not like Christ." He knelt, not as a vassal kneels in subservience, but as one kneels to lift a fallen child. "The punishment of the Almighty is on you. I can see and feel it."

For his insolence I would have torn his flesh and made his neck my chalice, but he was across the threshold and I could not reach to strike him.

"You have the debt of blood," he said to me. "Yes? You feel the bottomless thirst? The sun in the sky punishes you?"

"You know of this curse?"

"I have seen it before. You are *wampir* now, my lord—a sad and twisted parody of the Savior himself. As Christ died that we might live, you now live by the death of others. As His holy blood became a saving sacrament, your unholy blood is a pestilence, corrupting all who partake... and as He rose again at dawn, you shall die again each sunrise."

"These are only tales to frighten children!" I spat, but in my heart I knew he spoke the truth. I had become a thing of night terrors, existing only to wreck and destroy all that was good.

"Behold," he whispered. "Even your tears are red."

"What can I do? What is left for a creature such as I have become?"

"Repent. All is mutable, my lord. That is the last aspect of your Christian perversion. You change not, age not, and die not, but Christ is rebirth and renewal! Any grievous sin can be undone by His intervention. You have chosen this path, to be a human plague, but you can choose to return to the light as well. Admit your wrongdoing, beg the forgiveness of *your* Lord, and this change worked upon you can be undone."

For a moment, I gave myself hope, but I have always taken greater strength from truth, no matter how bitter. The abbot was wrong, I could feel it in my bones, in the very curse that seethed within me. Change was for men, as I had changed from an ally of the Turk to his bitterest foe, as my crown and country changed hands with each assassination and betrayal, as my own father bought his freedom from the Sultan with my captivity when I was but twelve years old.

No longer man, I could be only what I am. There is no redemption for me. I will not change, and neither will God.

I left Snagov burdened by bitter truths. I saw in the abbot's mirror my twisted countenance and I knew the hell-wolf I had become.

This news left me grieving and heavy at heart, but other news fired me again into rage. The monks had news that my own home, Castle Dracula, is infested by the usurpers. Intolerable! Those sacred walls, built by the bloodied hands of dissident Boyars whom I made haul stones until they dropped into the mercy of exhausted death, them and their wives in their Easter finery toiling for my glory. Am I now to let it rest in the hands of sniveling Radu and his Turks? Never!

Yet as I write this, I am cast down. All but three of my vassals are dead at the hands of the castle's defenders, and those three cower in madness, fit only to slake my thirst as I wander south. I, Dracula, who repelled the great Turkish invasion, have been flung from my home like a common mendicant.

It was by night we came, and disguised as a Turk I gained admission, slaughtered the door guards and raised the portcullis for my own small band, when I heard from behind me a chortle of laughter and a small round of mocking applause.

I turned to see two Turkish women, garbed for the seraglio, but standing in a doorway that opened to the courtyard.

I have faced untold battle terrors, I have supped in a grove of the impaled and slept easily afterward, but the sight of this pair boiled my heart with fright as nothing ever did in my living days. Yet I bit back this fright with the aid of my wrath and pride. If I am to be compelled to a sinful existence, then by my oath I shall choose my sins.

"Look," one crooned. "A native whelp has come to bark."

"Speak a Christian tongue!" I shouted in response. Though I could understand their courtly Turkish, I have often found value in an ignorant seeming.

"If you seek to insinuate your woeful self to the governor here, that place is taken," said the second, this time speaking German. "But here. Pledge us fealty and we shall give you the shelter of Invictus." With that, she shrugged her breast free and pierced it, letting blood well up like milk.

"I pledge fealty to no God, demon, or man, and least of all to any woman," I said. "The name Invictus will suit you poorly when I have shown your remains to the sun!"

The first laughed again. "He thinks 'Invictus' is your name," she trilled.

"Who was your sire, whelp?" asked the other. "Who made you a *ghul*?"

"God himself!"

They laughed again, and I chose that moment to strike.

There is little point in committing to ink exact means of my defeat. Suffice to say that the Turkish *strigoi* were swifter and stronger than I, though even now the notion of a woman's blows upon me causes my teeth to gnash. As they hurled me down the steps of my own residence, they spat upon me, told me I did not even deserve to be their slave, and that I should mark well the inevitable triumph of Invictus, the rulers of all the undead.

My surviving servants were those who fled in terror from those harlots of Invictus, whatever that might be. I write this on paper begged from the abbot, as I crouch in the crypt of some long-forgotten boyar.

The abbot said others were as I am, and the pair in my castle affirms it. This explains much. I had never paid heed to legends of *ghuls* in Turkey and *strigoi* here, but as I think back on my experience in Sultan Murad's court, and the nigh-unbelievable prowess of some who defended Sultan Mehmet's person during my night attack so many years ago... yes, it becomes clear. If such creatures existed, could they rule? Indeed, what force could stop them? Only their own might pitted against each other.

Yea, as in the world of men one king naturally strikes his brother, so in the world of the dead must one monster naturally compete with others of his ilk. I shall have to learn more of this 'Invictus'. I shall have to learn more of my nature. To do so I needs must follow those two beasts to their source. I must journey to Adrianople, the Ottoman capital.

When I have the answers I need, I shall return here and teach those bitches the abbot's lesson—that in this realm, all things may change.

· · ·

It is the year of the Christians' Lord 1480 and I have returned to reclaim my castle, at least.

How I have learned upon my five years' journey! The blood inside me cries, in anger or fear, at the sight of another of my damned ilk. By this means I have seen the thin film of *ghul*-kind who float on top of the human herd, like a skin of ice upon winter water. In the slums of Adrianople's bazaar I have seen them hide and scuttle, and in the depths of the Sultan's harem they plot and connive.

'Invictus' is simply a cabal among them, intervening itself wherever the mortals' governments have power. They have the Sultan's ear but not his heart, for his advisors are wise to their tricks and watch him closely for signs of blood madness.

As I peruse my old notes, I see that the abbot referred to this—that my blood would corrupt any who partook. This is literal truth, as my sniveling brother Radu has learned, to his regret. I came to his window in the form of a bat—another power of the blood that I have chiseled from God's miserly grasp—and forced myself upon him, not after the perverse fashion of Radu's sodomite master the Sultan, but in a way perhaps more ghastly yet. Now that my blood runs within him, his Reason begins to sway toward my will.

I have given him a month to dread my next visit, a month to hide in fear and sleep in a sealed chamber. Perhaps tomorrow night, or next week, he will let down his guard and a second taste will make love of me a fire within him. With the third taste, he will be a hollow man, living only to fulfill my whim and wish. I will never rule Wallachia again. My death is too widely known, and the secret undead lying in the Sultan's seraglio know what I have become. Nevertheless, my evil blood shall make puppet Radu dance upon my strings, not those of his turbaned lover.

The enslavement of men is not its sole use. I have learned how our kind beget. It is not through fumbling and uncertain rutting, but by an altogether more reasonable means. Those who die beneath my fangs can, should I choose it, return by my blood. It is hard, deathly difficult, but for one of true noble lineage the difficult is the commonplace.

I have a daughter now.

Or a wife, or a sister in damnation, it matters not. Human words fail for what Mara is to me. I met her in Adrianople, a beauty stolen from Afric shores and sold into Turkish bondage. Despite her charms and strength she was being sold on the cheap, for she had murdered a sailor who tried to woo her by force. I saw in her eyes a madness and hate equal to mine. Before purchase, we spoke.

"I was baptized into the Christian church," I told her. "What think you of that?"

Her answer was to spit in my face.

"I have killed many for much less offense than that. Are you afraid to die?"

"I would cherish death," she said in her broken Turkish.

"Yes, I believe you. If God, or whatever spirit you revere, came to you and gave you the sword of the angel of death... would you pick it up?"

"What mean you?"

"If you had a weapon to slay at will, unconcerned, would you wield it?"

"Who would not?"

"How would you use it?"

She did not answer with words, but her eyes narrowed and her gaze became distant as she looked at the streets about her.

"Would you kill them all? The children and the women as well?"

"The children would only grow to be vile, and the women would only swell and birth more evil."

"Then if God gave you a vial of pestilence, that could spread across all Europe and all Asia and your own nation, every nation across the sea... would you open the vial?"

She knew. She did not know my nature, but she knew my questions were not idle.

"Are you the Devil?" she asked, and her voice was all hope.

"I have been called his son," I said, and brought forth gold to purchase her.

I ignored the name she came with. I called her Mara—my little joke on the Sultan's mother.

Later, she did not sigh in pleasure when I bit her neck, as many do. Nor did she cry out as I became more savage and hacked at her to bring a faster flow, as most do. When I brought her back, she fed like an animal, as she has each night since. She is magnificent and shows no doubt, no regret, no uncertainty over what I have made her.

"Now, being this, the world makes sense," she says.

Together, alone, we returned to my homeland.

• • •

I have once more traveled to Tîrgoviste, and once more fed myself to Radu. As planned he becomes more servile. One more taste, for which he now begs, and my grasp on Wallachia will be all but complete. In the meanwhile, I entertain myself with Mara, showing her how to invert our Curse and make it serve us as power. As I taught, she asked me something.

WILLIAMS

"What is it like, to be a king?"

"It is very much like this," I said in reply. "You have power, and the right to do with it as you will. You have might and dominion such that no ordinary man can stand against you. Yet at all times you are aware of greater powers yet, which you must always fear and pacify."

"What powers? Do you mean God?"

"That is a simpleton's view. I mean popes and emperors, and the powers that support them. Even an emperor can be held hostage in his own home, should the people of his lands have an excess of anger and insufficient fear. Too, there is always another heir, and there are always those with power to gain by exulting that heir in your stead."

"I thought you killed all your rivals as children."

"I made a good try of it, but my relatives excel rabbits in fecundity. For rulers less practical than I, there are even more challengers."

"But who are the challengers to us, the damned of the night?"

This led me to thought. For in truth, if fear is the great ally of a ruler, how can ones so fearsome as we avoid the thrones of the world?

"I believe it is the changeability of the world," I said at last. "We are, by God's affliction, immutable. When the world changes, we are left behind, for maintaining power is always a wrestling match. The complacent ruler is not long for his throne. In my mortal days I was enthroned three times and thrice deposed, I first allied with the Turks and then became their greatest foe, I was baptized Catholic, raised Orthodox, converted back to Catholicism to marry, and died blaspheming God's name. I allied with the man who helped assassinate my father and was later betrayed when I soldiered beside his son against my own brother. By Hell, my brother Radu once defended his honor against Mehmed with sword and dagger, but now claims the throne as the Sultan's lover."

"Certainly there is truth to what you say," she said. "But are we doomed to be left behind by the world's mutability?"

"Not while our minds retain Reason. It is clear that God has taken half my Rational Soul, for the lusts and hungers of my Animal Soul are held much less in check thereby. Yet I still can learn, and therefore change, and so long as we can change we can hope. You and I, Mara, are drawn tight between our immutable bodies and our capacity to learn and think and begin anew. This tension would madden lesser souls, but we can draw strength and even grace from it, as a musician draws music from the taut string of his harp. We are given decades from which to view the world and learn its secrets, without men's distractions of aging and daily toil for bread. If we seize our punishment and make it a gift, while clinging tight to what power of thought we retain, we can be greater than any mortal—indeed, greater than any *ghul*!"

To demonstrate my point, I rose above her as a bat, circling the room before standing before her again.

"But to what purpose?" she asked.

"Must change have a purpose?"

"Indeed," she said. "Else all is chaos."

"What troubles you about chaos?"

Her eyes narrowed. "That what we call chaos is, from another perspective, the hidden hand of God."

Something in her tone chilled me. I sat, and peered into her eyes. "Explain."

"You were a Prince, a politician. You schemed and connived to alter the deeds of men. Whose actions are easier to mold, the man who is focused and driven, or the man who is confused and uncertain? You have been a soldier on the field. Which enemy is more readily tricked and destroyed, one with discipline and training? Or a muddled rabble?"

Though only a woman, Mara made great sense, and I shall forever be grateful for what I learned from her that night: That change must emerge from reasoned plan. If you move blindly, you are at the mercy of any who see you.

"Mara," I said. "I believe you have been sent by the Devil himself to aid me."

Tonight was the climax of all my plans, and it was delightful. Radu was shocked to learn that there were undead within the court his turbaned master sent to "attend" him. After the second drink of my blood, he was more than ready to believe my words about those two devilish concubines. At my direction, he took them by day. The pretty brace of them, upraised on stakes, were his offering to me.

"Ah," I said, looking upon them. "Is there any form so fair that it cannot be improved with the proper pedestal?"

I was not sure if they could see me, though I had done them the courtesy of cutting off their eyelids.

"I would love, dearly love, to hear what final words you might offer. Some defiant paean to Invictus? Some futile pleas for pity and release, spiced perhaps with promises of service? Would you abase yourself before Christ, or Allah, or some other virtuous deity? I think that perhaps you might be the type to suffer in dignified silence. My curiosity is deep... and yet, not that deep. No. It is petty to risk myself and my companions for such childish satisfactions. It is beneath me. You shall have no final say." I turned my face to Mara and said, "Mark well that you drink until the final speck is gone."

In all truth, my sole intention had been to kill them in a physically gratifying manner. Yet when I took the last sweet dram of blood from one, I felt a new stirring within me, the first caress of a new power. Eagerly, I attended it, and knew— knew as a dove knows the sky, as a dolphin knows the sea— that I could go deeper, could extinguish not only life, but that inner spirit which has no form in this world. I knew it would be delicious, that it would nourish me even as blood could not, and the instant I knew it could be mine, I decided it must be.

What does it mean? Can my power be so great that I can devour a soul—a spirit no longer immortal but only grist for my gluttony? It seems that what I felt could be naught else, yet if it is so then there is truly no permanence, even beyond this life! If what I felt was true, then the immortality promised by Christ the Redeemer and Mohammed the Prophet are both equal lies!

Are we truly spirits cast adrift, impermanent, sparks in the void? Have our great saints and leaders lied to us? Do no fires of Hell await the vicious, and is Heaven void of penitent souls? What God could make us so and yet see fit to punish an individual such as myself with perpetual existence?

Perhaps God is crueler than I. Perhaps the justice, promised by defiant monks from their dying stakes, is just an illusion more vicious than any torment I have devised.

Perhaps this world is all that there is. Perhaps God told me one thing but showed me another, spoke lying words to make me weak while giving my blood the tools of eternal strength...

When I completed my feed, Radu humbly beseeched me, that I might gift him again with my sanguine strength. No meek convert ever begged Christ's blood so prettily.

Who could resist such imploring? Especially since the gift chained a ruler to my will, utterly, mind and heart.

Through my poor weak little brother I sent away the guards and vassals and lackeys. I had tender virgins brought to slake my thirst (though, in truth, after my feast of Invictus I only killed them for the sake of appearances). And I sat upon my throne with my crown upon my brow, while the recognized Prince of Wallachia capered and clowned for my amusement.

My nation knows it not, but the Impaler Prince rules it once more.

WILLIAMS

Now the time has come to set aside this journal, diverting though it has been. I no longer need to echo my thoughts back at myself, for I have a world into which I can bellow commands. Tonight I fly back to Castle Dracula, to conceal these papers safely. Tomorrow, the return trip to Tirgoviste— and the dawn of a new state.

. . .

Not damned, not thrice damned, but four times cursed is the name of Dracula. Who else in history has been condemned to lose his throne not twice, but four times? Surely I am the plaything of God, or the Devil or malevolent Fortune.

I am wroth unto madness, but I am not surprised.

Radu, by himself, was a poor choice to rule. He prefers love to fear, which is wise for a minstrel but foolish for a Prince. His will was weak, as witnessed by the way the Sultan swayed him into unnatural vice, and I swayed him into unnatural service.

Furthermore, the bonds I placed upon him seem, from the perspective of experience, to have strained overmuch his Reason. I gave him wise commands to keep order in the kingdom and ensure the strength of his position, but a Prince must react moment by moment, not day by day (or night by night). He followed the letter of my commands and would have obeyed their meaning, had he only the mind to discern it. Blinded by his fixed and unhealthy love of me, he did not.

If I had a brighter ink than him with which to scrawl my intentions, I might have ruled by proxy. Now Basarab III claims the throne from Radu, with the aid of a fickle Sultan who suspects, no doubt, my unclean hand in this matter. Ah well.

My final and lonesome retreat is here, Castle Dracula, built by my ancestors and, by my command, rebuilt by my enslaved enemies. Through Radu I have ordered it abandoned and the roads to and from it—rough and ill-used at best—to be torn up and left as mud. A winter and a spring will suffice to erase them completely.

Here I can stay. There are several towns and villages close, within the night's flight of a bat, and I know that the gypsies will come through these mountains whether there is a road or not. I need fear no thirst.

I can rule a nation no longer. I cannot parley with my equals, I cannot mete out justice by daylight, I cannot command an army when the sun holds me frozen like death.

I will not retake my throne, tonight or ever, until the sun in the sky is no longer my foe. Instead, I turn myself to other matters. Before the conquest of the world, I would be well advised to conquer myself. As a man, I had total self-control, but as one of the *strigoi*, much eludes me. Here, alone in my keep, I will wrestle this beast within and break it to heel like my hunting-dog.

Ah, but first, there is a final matter to be settled and made orderly. I hear the royal carriage arriving. Basarab will no doubt be disappointed that Radu absconded with it...

Radu died better than I would have expected. First he arranged for his honor guard (a mere twenty troops! Even I had more aiding me when I fell) to walk directly into the trap I prepared. I'm delighted to have my larder so readily stocked.

Then he begged forgiveness for failing me, which lightened my anger somewhat. I told him that I would still give him the reward of eternal life (for that is how I have described our condition to him) if he could endure a test to prove his loyalty.

"Anything!" he promised.

Remarkably, he blanched only a little when I showed him the stake.

I have overseen the impalement of over twenty thousand men, women, children, and one donkey. Radu was different from all of them, and not solely because he was also my father's child. Radu went willingly, if not eagerly, and lasted as long as any. He said he could feel my blood within him, giving him strength, battling against the wounds that would end him. Fascinating. Was this literally true, or only a fancy of his poetic soul? To the very end, I promised him that after he breathed his last, I would restore him, and more, make him better than he had ever been. Mara and I knew the moment he perished— we could tell from the glaze of his eyes but more, his scent in our nostrils was no longer that of fresh prey, but only of a cold and unappetizing corpse. This too is a puzzling quality to investigate.

"Will you restore him now?" Mara asked me.

"Don't be foolish," I replied. "Feed of him as you will."

Book Two:
The Book of Blood

If all is flux and change, how is it that I find myself return-ing to the same places once, and again, and once more? As a mortal I gained my throne and lost it, and gained and lost twice more. Now undying, I nevertheless find my feet once more tread the cobblestones of Castle Dracula.

Perhaps change cycles like the seasons, with spring inevi-table after winter. Perhaps my own unholy nature—a permanent thing in an ever-changing world—draws me back time and again, here, to my home.

Yet even as I return to the same place, it is not the same nor am I. The walls, bulky and strong, are thick with vines and li-chen. Wooden roofs have fallen in and even mortar has given way.

The vault remains secure, however. That will do for the time being.

In that crypt I found my old writings, and I wince at the callow and preening peacock I was. To think I could rule, or that I had, or that any reign is aught but trickery and misdirec-tion in this vale of tears and deceit! It's laughable.

Who can truly reign when the choice between darkness and light is always and utterly within the human heart?

If the years have wrought their changes upon my castle, they have done so upon my spirit as well. Has it grown toward greatness like an oak from an acorn? No. Like the home of my body, the home of my heart is worn and decayed.

In life, as a man, I thought no glutting on blood and death could sate me, but my murderous sojourn in the lands of the Turks taught me otherwise. I killed nightly, striking high and low alike, as impartial as Fate, and I, Dracula, wearied of it. The physical bliss remains as rapturous as always, but even rapture stultifies the mind with incessant repetition.

I needed more. I needed something to make me think and feel, and to that end I traveled to Jerusalem in search of the Lancea Sanctum.

Should any reader beside myself one day peruse these pages, let me clarify that there is a vampire religion that reveres Longinus the centurion, holding him to be the representative of God's will among our kind. They have studied our condition and delved deep into the mysteries of our blood, and for a time I hoped their Theban sorcery would illuminate the dark questions in my mind.

They welcomed me eagerly—their leader had been Christian in life and despised the infidel Turks even in death, so a hero such as I was folded quickly to their bosom. Their initiations—by fire, temptation and the sword—were little compared to trials I have inflicted on myself.

Yet ultimately, I turned aside from the Centurion's path. They were able to push against the limits of our state, but only briefly, only in reprieve. Their changes to the world were miraculous, to be sure, but as impermanent as the dew which fades at sunrise. Further, they still trembled before God in the manner of those who secretly crave punishment for their sins. Now I regret turning aside from that wisdom, but then, I sought only the means to make my reprimand from God retribution unto Him in turn.

Perhaps Mara's blandishments led me astray, for she was ever disdainful of the Sanctified, as they called themselves. Yet I cannot blame a lowly woman (even an immortal one) for the poor decision I made. No, it was my hand that burned the bridge, my own willful tread that led me away from wisdom. That door is closed to me now.

Before I turned aside from them, their master had spoken, with the contempt that masks fear, of a band of pagans in the steppes who terrorized even the fearsome Tatars and whose blasphemies against God had lured demons to give them worldly power. In my madness and heresy, this sounded honey-sweet, and so to the mountains I went.

After a year of pointless searching and frenzied questioning of any who might know, I found the Circle of the Crone. It took another year to pass their tests and learn their litanies—madly rapid progress by their usual standards, but painfully slow to me. At last, I was initiated into the rituals of Cruac.

The pagans had much to teach, and their crescent symbol made me wonder much about that same symbol being used for Islam, but in the end I find their secrets as hollow as the Theban rites, and their so-called philosophy far more so.

It is certainly accurate to say that only through testing and trial can one overcome limitations, but the Passion of Christ proves this far more readily than the pains of Odin. The assertion that we are creatures of nature but beyond it will not stand rigorous scrutiny, for what else in the world of the earthly is as inalterable as we? Only the stars in their orbits show the same eternity, and to brag that we have their lofty matter within us is bold indeed for creatures who die every day and live only by the grace of suckling in need at the veins of the living.

Further, for all their claims about the infinite and absolute, the Acolytes can bend the world but lightly to their will, and only for a time, before it springs back with the vigor of a green twig.

Holding a boulder over one's head does not alter the nature of the stone, and to say that it is higher or lighter is to attribute to rock that effort which wearies one's own sinews. Both the Theban and the Crescent paths are strong, and not to be mocked nor taken lightly, but ultimately they share they same failing: They can deform the world, but not truly change it. They write their power with air on the wind, and in an instant it fades.

To truly make the changes I seek, I must delve within and work my wonders upon myself.

This is the reason for my return to Castle Dracula, with Mara still at my side. While she has myriad flaws—most of which I counted as virtues when I gave her the dubious gift of our condition—disloyalty is not one of them. Yet can steadfastness be a virtue in a creature immune to change? Does she remain with me from devotion, or the inertia to which our kind is inevitably prone? I know I will get no meaningful answer if I ask her, any more than I would receive a thoughtful reply quizzing a dog about its faithfulness. Mara hunts and kills and is a well-honed predator, but she will never look deeper into the world than at her next source of blood.

• • •

I have progressed with the great work.

Theban sorcery is predicated on the submission of self to another—to the higher power of the blood and to Longinus himself, who is a dark Christ to his followers and revered beyond all reason. Cruac is in some sense the opposite, the submission of another to the self—but self as blood wielder, self as monster. The Sanctified sacrifice the man to the Beast, and the Acolytes sacrifice the world to it, but these are ultimately temporary sacrifices because the Beast cannot change, while world and man always must.

I have found a third way.

Both those practices move on straight lines, but any leader can tell you that the real course to power is often a crooked path. I have found that path, and it winds and binds the very essence of what I am. With its coils, I can sacrifice the Beast to the Beast.

Observe. What are the qualities of the *strigoi,* the *ghuls,* the vampires?

CRAVING is the first quality. We are incomplete creatures, robbed of something essential by our curse, and to offset this lack we take blood. We take sustenance from blood, we take meaning from blood and we take our only unalloyed pleasure in blood. The emptiness and hunger defines what we are. If we do not feed, we shrivel into nothingness.

STAGNATION is the second quality. We do not age, we resist illness and poison, we change ourselves only with the greatest exertion, we breed more of our ilk only through the most grievous straining against what can laughably be called our "nature." This is why fire and the sun are our banes, because they cleanse, renew and give life. Life is the only thing that can overcome our suspension from time.

UNREASON is the third quality. Our Rational Souls are crippled by our transformation, leaving us animals with a man's contempt for our bestiality. This curse makes us craven against our elders and vicious to all others, makes us cringe or rave, makes us act on instinct and not by proper thought.

These are the chains that bind us. Yet each link can be forged with another into a key for the third.

To overwhelm my first, fiercest and most enduring flaw, the thirst that makes me murder, the hunger which makes me unclean... this is the challenge, to coil upon the blood and squeeze that need into submission. What allies can I find in the fight against this need?

Stagnation is my best and most powerful ally. Already my body is built to change not, already its power resists time and decay. It is but necessary to marshal this prowess against a new foe, against the thirst which, when thwarted, dries my skin and withers my sinew. Stagnation calls me already. I need but heed the call on my own terms.

Blood is not mere sustenance for me, of course. It is not only the gross physical matter of the sanguine fluid, but also the stuff of soul which beats through it—the passion for love that warms it, and the passion of hate which boils it. Blood is not solely blood but also vigor, strength, and it is for this purpose that my angry unreason can be harnessed. The rage, the heat, it is within me already and need not be borrowed from without. Let the Animal Soul bite and suck itself and thereby be sated.

The second challenge is the terror of the flame and that penultimate flame, fiery Phoebus above. Fire is the principle of change and therefore my blight and anathema. Yet am I not the Dragon? Is flame not my very breath? Am I not the fire's kin?

Fire consumes and grows as it is fed, and do I not as well? I turn to the craving, turn to the red thirst, and know what it is to be fire, to crave all, to have an overwhelming passion to feed. I recognize fire's hunger in my hunger and fire's nature in my nature.

If the spirit of fire is one of hunger, I know also that it is one of wrath—heedless, remorseless, caring not that the destruction of its fuel inexorably starves it away. This madness also has is cousin within me, in my unreasoning Beast. If I turn rage on rage, what merely natural flame can overcome the wrath of the All Powerful?

The third and most insidious opponent is one that dwells, lover close, within me. It is my own damned nature, my unreason, my urge to live in an endless crimson now of slaughter and animal fulfillment, heedless—indeed, incapable of considering!—the demise my madness invites.

This battle seems doomed to stalemate, for my enemy is very much my self, perhaps my self of selves. What offsets this? My lacks. My emptiness. My thirst. Oh, compared to what I am missing, what I have is very weak indeed.

Too, my own eternity bolsters me in this fight, for while the Beast is always and essentially a creature of the Now, I am forever composed to be a creature of Forever. In the blank depths of eternity, the rage of an instant, no matter how fierce, is ultimately but a spark. I can stretch a rope between my stagnation and my wrath, and c l i m b cross the abyss upon it.

It is demonstrated thus. What force is stronger than the curse of God above? The strength of two divine curses combined.

Such is the philosophy of the matter. Now to test my airy thoughts against the fire and the blood.

• • •

God is cruel.

I read the pages that lie beside this one and see my pride once more pushing higher my hopes. Indeed, my theory of Coils has proven correct, and my explorations have been profoundly promising. I had dared think that the mercy of the Lord is truly boundless and that even a wretch such as I, a murdering fiend of the stripe I have been, might find freedom from His curse in the fullness of time.

I thought and hoped and dared dream of becoming more than a bloodied night-taker, and then Fortune, God's mastiff, growls and bites.

My castle home has been invaded.

The intruders are no mere gypsy band, of the type I have affrighted away before. Nor are they a troop of soldiers, who could easily be my prey for long months. No, they are but three, traveling alone and lightly armed. Surely they should hold no fear for terrors like Mara and myself?

Yet they built four fires at sunset, large and bright from the seasoned timber of old doors and outbuilding walls. They built their fires and slept in the middle of them, despite the warmth of the night.

One fire is sufficient to repel wolves and vermin. Their intrusive camp is set so that none may enter without passing between two fires—something many *strigoi* would be loath to do.

I gave them their first night. I watched them from beyond the fire's glow. Each in turn kept guard. Each in turn I examined closer, in bat form, relying on the Coils to offset my instinct to flee the flames.

The first, who took the early watch, is a scholar. To the eye, a lean man of monkish mien, elderly—perhaps as old as fifty. He had no cleric's tonsure, but his back bore the bend of a habitual reader. Perhaps a Jew but more likely French or Italian. Upon his face he bore some of the waspish suspicion those nations lend their people. He carried a dagger in his belt, and kept a crossbow nearby, loaded. Yet when I flew past him as a bat, he peered at me with great suspicion, and even drew forth a small and polished mirror with which to inspect me. I believe I flew off before he could sight me.

The midnight shift saw the rise of a woman of middle age, perhaps twenty or so, heavyset and with a complexion that spoke of a racial miscegenation. She carried a sword with strange decorations—a straight edge but with a tassel on the pommel and oddly curved letters inscribed upon the blade. He clothes were of Eastern silk. Among her possessions was a spiked buckler, which she kept close to hand.

The third is a Saxon, of the same stripe who so plagued me from their tidy, industrious towns during my reign. Barely of age, he was a strapping youth with a mane of blonde hair and a fuzzy wisp of beard already decorating his chin. He wore a chain shirt and carried a sword with a confidence that told me he himself had put the notches upon its metal.

How pleasant I would have once found it, to arise from sleep to the sound of screams.

Before repose last night, I gave serious thought to the entertainment of my guests (who did not, at that time, understand that they had that honor). While a strike by night appealed to my Animal Soul, and to Mara, I felt compelled to give them a better chance. How can I ever transcend what I am, if I succumb to any fleeting thirst for viciousness? I therefore decided this evening to greet them in a style befitting my station.

One who knows me only by the written boasts of decades past, recorded in these frail pages, would think I meant a banquet meant to thrill and impress—or else a feast of blood meant to repel and terrify them. No, now I am not as I was. I am a philosopher now. I have a simple existence fit for one who seeks treasures that are grasped with the mind, not held in the hand. I sent Mara to the village to procure some victuals last night (she is a marvel of pragmatism on such missions), while I took measures to defend those treasures I do possess—my writings, my thoughts and the records of my studies.

From the bellows I heard upon waking, I was forced to conclude that our guests had attempted to enter my library. A pity, yet not unexpected. I asked Mara to watch unseen, while I went out through the old postern and crept around, that I might present the appearance of a traveler at journey's end.

The shouts were those of the Scholar, with the Woman setting his broken leg. The Saxon aided the endeavor by sitting upon the patient's shoulders, lest his thrashing undo the Woman's work.

Entering, I steeled myself, that the scent of blood would not arouse me. "Good evening," I said.

The two whole of limb looked up at me.

"You seem to have fallen upon some mischance," I said.

The youth spoke in German. "The stairs gave way beneath him."

"How unfortunate! I was told this old place was unsafe..."

"And I, that it was abandoned." The Scholar had, with impressive effort, composed himself. "Might I ask your name, stranger?"

"I am Paolo Jaroslavic," I said. "I have been awarded this property for recent service to the crown."

"I am Hermes," he said, pronouncing it in the French fashion. "These are my associates Anoushka and Ivor." Ivor was the Saxon.

"I am grieved that my first guests should be in such straitened need, but I can, at the least, offer you the rude hospitality of a meal, with perhaps some wine to dull the pain of your leg."

"We would not be beholden," Ivor said in rough Latin.

"Nor would I hold you indebted," I said. "My country has a tradition of hospitality. It is a matter of honor."

"We prefer to see to our own needs."

"Do you not trust my taste and my table?"

He shrugged. "It is you who say so."

"You damnable whelp! I find you squatting like bandits upon my property, I offer you the grace of my hospitality in your time of need and I am repaid with the uppity bleating of a stiff-necked child? I'm not sure if I should demand satisfaction or look for your father to have him cuff your ears!"

Ivor was stung and growled, verily growled like a beast, as he reached for his weapon, but the woman Anoushka restrained him.

"Please forgive my comrade," she said. "I am sure you meant us no harm, even as he meant you no disrespect. We would be delighted to share your meal."

"You would be wise to heed your elders," I told Ivor. He muttered something in his native tongue, something I didn't catch. I am trying, truly trying, to resist my more violent impulses, but this lad seemed determined to tempt them.

I claimed the simple meal that Mara, hidden, prepared for them. They, with some trepidation and suspicious sniffing, consumed it. I demurred, saying that I had eaten earlier, in the village, and was merely bringing back supplies for my own later meals. I caught Hermes peeping at me in his mirror several times, but with some effort I made firm my reflection.

I begged them to regale me with tales of their travels, and was met in turn with questions about myself and how I had come to possess the fortress. I spun them a plausibly dull fabric of lies—my knowledge of courtly life has rusted over the decades, but surely it cannot change much and is still the usual swamp of treason and selfishness. I presented myself as a loyal warrior whose honesty was inconvenient at court, and who was therefore "rewarded" with an obscure and run-down fiefdom. I said my escort had abandoned me after a dispute in a brothel, and mentioned in passing that a squad of soldiers was soon to follow, with builders after them.

The trio exchanged glances at that.

With my tale told, I again asked them what business brought them so far off the major trade routes, and how so varied a group had come to travel together.

With a shrug, Hermes the scholar replied.

"We call ourselves the Circle of Three Sides," he said, "And we are seekers after esoteric truth."

"That sounds fascinating," I replied, pouring more wine. "Pray, tell me more."

"Are you aware of the history of this castle?"

"It was built by the great crusader Dracula, was it not?" I could not resist the temptation.

"By his ancestors, but it is the Impaler's involvement that interests us. Many years ago, at Easter, he ambushed some rival Boyars, clapped them in chains and worked them to death at sword point, thickening the walls here to resist Turkish cannon."

"I believe I've heard the tale."

"Have you heard more recent tales of a haunting spirit? They say it takes the form of a bat, or a wolf, or a ravenous black shadow. The villages nearby live in terror, saying it flies and hunts by night."

"Hunts for what?"

"For blood," Ivor said.

There was a pause before I replied, "By merciful heaven. Surely this is just a peasant superstition?"

"We mean to find out. Blood can call to blood. Unholy shades may uneasy lie." Hermes was keeping his counsel guarded, but Anoushka had become loquacious. I had noticed her tendency to blush and look away every time I met her gaze, yes, look away and sip at her wine. I made sure to look often.

"How can such a thing happen in a Christian nation?"

"It can happen anywhere. When the shape of the land, and the tears of the dead, and the stories of the people all lie in a proper configuration... that is where the dragons nest, that is where..." She said something in a strange language, and then Hermes made sharp reply in the same tongue. She flushed again, this time I think with shame.

Interesting.

"Dragons? The Prince of whom you spoke, 'Dracula'—his name means 'Son of the Dragon' does it not?"

"Or 'Son of the Devil'," said Ivor.

"The Dracula I know is a patriot, a loyal defender who protected Christendom at great cost."

"At the cost of murdering twenty thousand helpless prisoners and nearly a like number of his own people!"

"Those stories are spread by the Germans," I said. "He taxed the Saxons as he did the Wallachians and they hated him for it, so they spread tales that he committed many atrocities." I shrugged. "It is all in the past, is it not?"

"If an evil is deep enough," Hermes said, "It can echo on through time, repeating until it is stopped." He looked me right in the eye as he spoke thus, and I found myself unnerved. Yet it would be a poor Prince who let any fanciful worry show.

"How would you go about purifying my land, if it is haunted by sorrow as you say?"

Hermes shook his head. "Too early to tell."

• • •

It is the first time in several days that I have been able to sit, write, and gather my scattered thoughts.

I was unimpressed but unsurprised by the repayment of my hospitality. The next nightfall, they were suspicious of me, as I had known they would be. They had forced entry into my library during the day, and were braced for siege. Bright torches lay in each stone windowsill, while a roaring fire sent smoke up the chimney. They had smashed down the door after getting to the top of the broken stairs somehow, but as a replacement they leaned a sturdy table in the empty doorway. I'm sure it was well braced.

They couldn't hold me at bay forever, but neither did they need to. By dawn, the sun would oppress me and they would be able to flee. I could pursue them at night, but such a chase would be fraught with perils and uncertainty.

No, it was clearly time to parlay. My only fear was that they had harmed my works.

Matt Hughes

"What knavery is this?" I demanded. "I serve you food from my table and grant leave to sleep 'neath my roof, and as reward you burgle my home? For shame!"

"You have no position from which to decry us, you *wampir* fiend!" Ivor, of course.

"Ah. You've read my papers and added spying to your list of offenses. Tell me, if those same documents had proven me harmless, would you be so cavalier about your transgressions?"

"What does it matter?"

"It matters because an action is right or wrong when it is taken, not when a selfish guess proves right."

"Selfish? We have come here at great peril to confront you! We have come here to free the countryside of your curse, to untwist the cruel knot you have tied upon the nature of the land!"

"Bold words from a stripling hiding behind barricades. Is your plan to bruise me by cowering, or to wound me with self-righteous language?"

He howled, by all Heaven! My anger had called to his and touched him quick. I heard the sounds of struggle within the library and, though it grieves me to confess it now, I rejoiced at the thought of hurting him.

What a splendid show he made, flinging aside the barricade and leaping like a spring buck the gap in the staircase. He charged clattering down the steps at me, sword raised, eyes mad, and I met him steel on steel.

He was stronger and quicker, as I'd guessed, but his skill surprised me. I did not expect him to have the discipline that expertise requires, yet he had leashed his fury with study. I fought defensively and immediately began giving ground. From the doorway, Anoushka was shouting at him to cease but he was battle-mad and would not have heeded

God Himself.

I know that madness well.

Why did I not give in to my own unreason, spending each last drop of strength to overcome him? Is it because I have recovered some greater measure of that which makes me Man? Or is it because I simply did not think I could best him?

It matters not. I had a plan.

I made a good show of fierceness but gave way, gave way, luring him in even as I once lured the Sultan's army to disaster. We turned a corner at last, each using the stone edge as a shield around which to strike, then a few steps further and no one from the library could see us.

Mara flew above him as a bat and fell upon him as a woman, but a woman bedecked with claws fit for a tiger. She has the skill of rapid change. She tore his flesh and bit his neck and that rich crimson scent filled the air.

The lust for murder filled me and I wanted nothing in the world so much as to drink the whelp dry, but I did not. Perhaps only to prove to myself that I could resist, but that is something, is it not?

I disarmed him and reined in Mara. She obeyed, albeit grudgingly.

"You crave my blood?" I asked him. "Taste, then, that which you longed to shed."

He resisted, but Mara wrenched open his mouth that I might poison him with love of me. Then I seized him by the ear and hauled him back to where his comrades might see him.

"Were I the fiend you think me," I said, "Would I have left unspilled one drop of this odious Saxon's blood?"

Anoushka had her buckler and sword ready, and Hermes aimed his crossbow from the doorway's edge, but they did not fire.

"I am trying to escape my curse! I am trying to become more than I am! I am trying to earn God's forgiveness for my transgressions—yea, and if you but read the papers you have stolen, you will see that I speak the truth!"

"Let him go!" cried Hermes. "Release him or we will burn your work!"

I was relieved that they had not already done so, but concealed it. "Is this how you carry out your noble quest for knowledge? By ruining it like the Muslims at the library of Alexandria? I have documented my great labor of atonement, and you would have that be all for naught? Your hypocrisy disgusts me. Whether you claim to love knowledge or hate destruction, you are a liar to me and I think to yourself."

WILLIAMS

There was a pause.

"I fear I have misjudged you," Hermes said at last, and from her hiding place Mara laughed—the first I've heard her laugh in decades, since she saw a pregnant woman get her legs broken by a runaway carriage. I hushed her.

"I fear you have," I said. "I cannot abide the abuses you have shown my hospitality. Get out, leave immediately, and do not return under pain of death."

"You have little right to demand..."

"I have every right! This is my land, my home, and if you care little for that, I have all the power I need to halt, enslave or destroy you. Oh broken limbed scholar, how will you descend from your lofty retreat? Ivor here is now too weak, too battered to lift you, though I suppose your Anoushka might be able to lower you by rope. Did you bring rope?"

"We did!"

"Splendid! Now you can hang yourselves, and be spared such punishment as I would design. For if you would hold out, how long can you last without provisions? If you would flee by day, how far do you think you would get by next nightfall? One lame man, one direly injured, on ruined trails, without horses... oh, did you carry your horses up into the library with you? No? Such a pity."

"Your papers..."

"Burn my papers and be damned! What I have discovered once in twenty years I can recreate in ten, or five. You, however, can only carry out that threat once before its protection is denied you."

"Let them go," said Anoushka, and there was aught in her tone that gave me pause. No bravado, no force, no diplomat's hauteur, just... resignation.

With, mayhap, a breath of desire underneath it?

"You say 'them,' let 'them' go and not 'let us.' I am intrigued, most intrigued, by that 'them'."

"I will stay. I will be a hostage to their behavior."

I narrowed my eyes. "Clasp a viper to my bosom? Invite an assassin to my very chamber? You must think me no end a fool."

"How dare you speak of her that way!" cried Hermes, and I then knew who loved whom. "She is the best of us, the highest and most noble, her honesty is without equal!"

"Ah, the first among thieves, liars and traitors. You'll forgive me if I do not rush to accept her."

She cast her shield and weapon down unto the cobblestones beneath the stairs.

"Surely the great Dracula can secure one woman. If all three of us were no threat to you, what can one be?"

"You would remain here, my prisoner, to protect this braggart and that sneak?"

"They are not those things to me," she said.

I narrowed my eyes. "Do you not fear that I will slake my blasphemous thirst upon your lovely throat?"

"I…" Yes, that 'lovely' made her words uneasy, it made her blood rise, I knew. "Of course I do. But I believe in you."

"You…?"

"I understand what you want, what you're trying to do, and I believe in it. I believe it's possible, that you can do it. I want to help you defeat your curse. I want to help you heal."

"You extend your aid to one befouled by God?"

"Universal mercy is unbounded," she said. "If you truly repent, if you truly want to step off your evil path, I believe you can."

"Will you pledge your life upon the good behavior of your companions?"

The scholar would have spoken, but her gesture silenced him.

"If it should come to that, my life will be forfeit. But it will not. They are good men. They will keep their word."

I narrowed my eyes and she beseeched me yet again.

"I know how much you desire this. It is clear in every line you have written."

Perhaps, until that moment, I did not know myself how much I dared hope for redemption.

That was three nights ago. Two days past, Ivor and Hermes set off stumbling and, I expect, cursing my name and weeping for the lost side of their circle.

As for Anoushka, I have had two nights to become increasingly fascinated.

She is a half-caste from far India, the byblow of a snake-charmer and a temple dancer who was orphaned by shipwreck at age twelve, rescued by an Italian trade vessel, and raised to the age of twenty in a Venetian nunnery. She fled the convent after wounding the local prelate when he came to hear the nun's confessions and made amorous advances to her. She left Venice for Padua and there met Hermes, who recognized a previously hidden talent for comprehending the occult.

Hermes' eye was sharp, I happily grant him that. Anoushka readily grasped my theory of Coils and has suggested my progress to date is partially due to Castle Dracula. She has explained to me, with great clarity, the means by which the shape of the land sculpts the lives of those who dwell upon it. Not merely in the rude sense of affecting military events or influencing the growth of crops, but in an unseen and magical dimension as well. When the land is wholesome, the people prosper.

I asked her what the effect was if the land belonged to something undead, and she could not meet my eyes.

Is this some new level to God's depravity? That my curse falls not only on me, but upon everyone nearby?

No, I cannot blame the Lord for what my hands have wrought. It was not God who picked the freshest, youngest necks from which to feed, it was I. God did not give Mara the tools to avenge herself on mankind eternally—it was I, seeking a sister in carnage and creating something that has only become more depraved, more vicious, less human with each passing year.

Anoushka believes that there is a reason for all, and that even the vilest of us can be redeemed.

"Think of it," she said. "What great fortress of good would this castle be, if it was here that you were saved? Here that you defeated your curse? I believe that the greatest evils are twisted virtues—the rape that takes the act of love and makes it an act of hate, or the priest who abuses the faith of his congregants to enrich and debase himself. So, too, can the greatest virtues arise from redeemed evil. What is the Christian story, if not the inversion of suffering, treachery, callousness and death into forgiveness, transcendence, acceptance and life? If you can save yourself, you who were so degraded as to merit judgment directly from heaven, what mortal could despair?"

Her words are a balm, soothing the fever of doubt which plagues my hopes.

• • •

I nearly killed Mara.

More, I nearly destroyed her, I nearly feasted upon her soul as I did so long before. I would have. I should. She is a cancer, a plague upon the land, a vexation to mankind.

She is all that I wanted her to be and I regret the day I clapped eyes on her chain-clad, wretched body.

I nearly killed Mara but she is too strong for me. While I delved into the secrets of the Crone's circle and the Centurion's believers, she bent her study to the more blatant strengths of the blood. At the time I felt no small contempt, thinking that she had chosen the easier path, a fit course for an unlettered female slave.

Tonight my arrogance is my punishment. Mara dealt me to the ground with the ease of a parent cuffing an angry child. "I could never hurt you," she said, "You who gave me all that I am. But neither will I humbly suffer your blows. You have forgotten what you are, have become drunk on sweet Christian lies, but their liquor is not what you need. You are a creature of blood."

Mara has put her *ghul* lips to Anoushka and made that poor gentle thinker into a creature like ourselves. When I demanded an explanation for this crime, her answers mocked me like an echo of my own words.

"How could you do this?" I asked, and she showed her white teeth behind dark lips and said, "It is you who showed me the way."

"But why? What does it gain you?"

"Yours was not the only interest roused by her words. She said the greatest evils are perversions of good." She chuckled, low in her throat. "Consider her an experiment to prove it thus, great philosopher."

"I am trying to atone! She wished only to help me!"

"Surely her urge to aid you in your atonement will be all the keener, now that she is your granddaughter in defilement."

That was when I struck her, and she struck me, and our exchange ended with her holding me down on a table and peering into my eyes.

"My lord and Prince," she whispered. "Either you are right or you are wrong. Either God can forgive you or you cannot be forgiven. If you are right, then your weak and sentimental new friend will be the first fruit of your efforts to heal us all. If you are wrong, then we are nothing but damnation made manifest, the First Sin made flesh and given reign to torment all sinners. If that is so, I can think of no act more apt for my station than to corrupt so well-meaning a soul."

With that, she leapt into the air and flitted away as a bat.

Thirty years ago, I would have pursued her. I would have spared no least slim shaving of effort, existing solely to avenge her insult to me.

Tonight, I comforted Anoushka instead.

• • •

It is several nights since Anoushka's change and, while tears still frequently wrack her, I think there is a courage in her that will give her the strength to travel.

For now, just as I have reclaimed my home, it is time to leave it. Anoushka insists that Hermes has the answers we seek, and that once he sees what was inflicted upon her he will be driven to help me find my cure. Therefore, we are off to the great university in Paris.

It grieves me to leave my home, but I will be taking a part of it with me. By bearing my native soil with me, I hope to maintain a link to the lands of my birth.

I find myself of two minds. While I feel an urge to remain in my den, feeding at leisure off the people I know, I fear that is the counsel of my static curse. The contrary urge—to see great Paris, to delve into the secrets gleaned by the world's greatest scholars, to test myself against my curse in the very heart of Europe—that is my own courage speaking. That is my drive to become greater, to learn more, to overwhelm any difficulty.

To be a man.

Book Three:
The Book of the Temple

What a glorious shock it has been to return. To see the land, changed but the same. To see the familiar outlines of my home, now scratched and sculpted by age. To dig forth again the musty pages of my journal and read, with laugh and wince, the thoughts I felt were so profound, my worthy gift for the ages.

"To be a man." Hah!

To be a man is to be false, quivering, cowardly and inconstant. To be a man is to fear death and flee. All the greatness mankind has achieved has been accomplished despite his natural tendencies, not because of them. Humans have within them a soul, celestial spirit unchanging, and when that whelms their Animal impulses they can touch resplendence.

How much greater am I, unalterable by nature? Yet still, my greatness must come from defying what I merely am, in pursuit of what I still might be. My challenge is to grow, change, set aside foolishness and embrace new ideas.

To balance these things—the man, the monster, the angel, the animal—is to become greater than all of them.

Anoushka was relieved to return here, poor pet. Paris taught her too much of herself—the intensity of flesh and abandon overwhelmed her. It is a pity she retains the goodness to agonize over her actions, but I am not surprised. Reading my old notes shows me that once I was the same, once I wailed and beat my breast, using remorse to justify cowardice and letting a fear of doing evil keep me from finding the very treasures of existence.

Love. Yes, I have found love.

I saw Lisette, a meek scholar's daughter, peering over the wall of the convent school in Paris, her eyes ignorant but somehow not pure and her hair, ah! A touch of the noontime sun I am forever denied.

How perfect that I first saw her on sanctified ground, trying so desperately to see what lay beyond it.

Now she knows.

Sweet Lisette, taught by her father to always wish to learn. What delights and terrors will we teach each other in the coming years, decades, centuries? A fruit plucked at the peak of ripeness, sixteen, the age at which a woman first spies the shadows cast by moral reality. Before Lisette learned even trepidation for them, she was plunged into the deepest darkness and has made her peace with it.

It took me fifty years!

While my darling was the most comely reward of my trip to great Paris, she was not the most illuminating. Fouchard, my friend, why must you slumber? Hideous, wise and powerful, Fouchard had learned the fullest mysteries of the Lancea Sanctum. At first my enemy, his own wisdom was his undoing. I told him of the Coils—aye, under duress I told him all I knew. A lesser man would have destroyed me, destroyed the truth rather than hang his head at the edifice of lies he had so carefully built and tended.

Fouchard was stronger. He heard my words and saw the ideas behind them. He realized the emptiness of his faith and cast it off, the weight of a century's belief, but he threw it aside like a paper ribbon when the real path opened before him.

He studied with me, but taught me far more than he learned. Between him and Anoushka, I found myself lagging behind as often as I lunged ahead. Nourished by Fouchard's knowledge, the Coils grew like spring ivy.

Now, Fouchard has fallen into the slumber of madness—a curious thing, spoken of in Jerusalem but which I had heretofore not seen. Is it a trick of our stagnation, overwhelming even movement until the changefulness of the world can exhaust it? Or is it a dream of unreason, separating us from the most fundamental knowledge of the world around us?

It is most likely a collusion of the two, an entwining that plays to both weaknesses, as I play to both strengths with the Coils. This makes it unlikely to be overcome in that fashion, though who is to say what is possible or not? Before me, Fouchard saw dawn as an insurmountable obstacle.

Fouchard slumbers in the catacombs of his homeland, too proud to take my offer of protection, and I cannot blame him. Even when flight is safer, who can abandon his home and hold his head high? Besides, if he were to leave Paris with me, the suspicions of his enemies—those who would wrest his authority within the Sanctified from him—would be more than confirmed.

Sadly, while they could not move against him, nor against me while he could shield me, his absence necessitates my own. The Sanctified have no patience for apostates, and by demonstrating that the punishment they gladly accept can be mitigated I have certainly been branded as such.

Thus, my journey home becomes a honeymoon for Lisette, though we are closer than any mortal nuptials could bind us. It is a retreat from a crusade by backwards necro-theologians. Most importantly, it is a chance to survey my domain.

Castle Dracula is losing the occult might it once had. I feel the tie waning, and I would know the reason.

Both Lisette and Anoushka find the castle gloomy. Lisette plants bright flowers, which she can only see flickering by lampglow or faded by moonlight. Anoushka flings herself into sorrow unresisting, draped in mourning garb, conversing mainly with animals and feeding only on the lowliest of vermin.

• • •

It is dusk, and some troupe of wagons approaches—gypsies if I am fortunate, for they rightly fear my name and domain. But these carriages seem more sober than those of the Romney—more like hearses.

I write these notes and will conceal them before sallying out to spy upon them. Lisette is to stay in the fortress while I prowl them as a bat, and Anoushka asks the animals what they have seen.

If they are coming here, why? Has the Inquisition finally turned its eyes east? Or is it warriors of the Spear, come from Paris to punish me? Surely neither is likely. The church has little care for Wallachian peasants, and the *strigoi* of Paris see no reason to depart their secure, sedate homes. Yet, if not them, who is it? There is little reason else to travel these obscure and treacherous roads.

It fruits nothing to wonder. Soon, I shall know.

• • •

How strange is Fate? The caravan is a clique of five *strigoi* with their several aides and a herd of two dozen feed-slaves. Most amusingly, their leader is Mara.

After transforming Anoushka and leaving me, she fled north to Germany and beyond, asserting a place as a *wampir* in Prague. Although they were hesitant to accept her initially, she persuaded them by destroying two rivals—using, I suspect, the rudimentary Coils I had taught her before her departure. Certainly that occult knowledge was essential when it came time to lead her little band of monsters. They came together under her dominion and she attempted to show them the Coils. Succeeding but indifferently in their studies, they set out to my castle, hoping that its occult inclining would reveal what she could not.

In recounting her tale, Mara did not mention any notion that I might be in residence at my keep, nor did she refer to any persecution in Prague. Her journey was not kind, and her once immutable flesh is altered. Her beauty has coarsened somehow, and human expressions sit imperfectly on her visage. Still, I suspect both hope and fear contributed to their decision to travel.

The question, however, is clear. What am I to do with Mara, her followers, Lisette, and Anoushka? A passel of twenty-some humans to bleed is all very well, but the eight of us cannot feed on a thin two-dozen for long. The folk of the villages are now afraid of the monsters in the keep, frightened still and motionless. If our predation becomes worse, they will be frightened into action, most likely flight, which only leaves the hunting poorer and the situation more dire.

Lisette is young enough to feed solely on animals, but I would not inflict that privation on my dearest. For that matter, both Anoushka and I possess the Coil to survive without human blood, but doing so is a fierce stress and strain upon any *ghul* of our stripe. No, there are too many of us here, and some will have to go.

I doubt I could eject Mara and her companions by force, even if she remains unwilling to harm me. Too, there is the matter of the Coil scraps they have learned.

They are eager for the deeper teaching I can offer, and it would be good to be once more in command.

I shall have to discuss this matter with the three of them. Lisette, my love; Anoushka, my conscience; and Mara, the mirror of my deadly ambitions.

(What follows was recorded by scholarly Anoushka, but the others of us have looked upon it and agreed that it contains the proper substance of our speech.)

VLAD: I must confess to some surprise that you would return here, Mara.

MARA: Where can a child turn, if not to her father?

VLAD: I am only your father in damnation, and I am nothing of any sort to those wretches you have dragged in your wake.

MARA: You could be. You could be everything to them.

ANOUSHKA: Why would he want to?

MARA: Why would he keep you by his side, puling and weak and mewling of good and evil? Why would he bring some honey-haired infant who lacks even the wit to snivel?

LISETTE: Damn you for a...

VLAD: That will do, Mara. You do your arguments no favor by insulting those you ought persuade. Anoushka is a mind of the highest caliber, despite her sex. She has done more with the Coils than you could do if you labored at them from the Fall of Adam through the Judgment Day. As for Lisette, she is beloved to me in a way you cannot know. For that alone, she deserves your respect.

MARA: You do your arguments no favor by belittling me!

VLAD: This is my home, and I shall entertain who pleases me. You, Mara, violated my hospitality when you laid violent hands upon Anoushka, my guest. Why should I shelter you again?

MARA: Perhaps because you lack the strength to enforce my exile. I've struck you to the floor once. I don't want to do it again, but I will if I must.

ANOUSHKA: Bold words for one outnumbered!

MARA: At a word, my followers would sunder that door and slay you all.

VLAD: No, they would begin to sunder that door, and you would not survive to see whether they won victory or slaked our thirst. I will not be threatened, and I will not have my people be threatened.

• • •

With that, I seized a brand from the fire and held it before her. She flinched back while the skin of my hand sizzled and spat. That cowed her, the fire, and her fear of it, and my courage. But I knew in my heart that her threat was genuine, and all my bluster hollow.

• • •

MARA: What I did, I did because it is my nature, my purpose.

ANOUSHKA: That is no excuse, and barely an explanation! You take as your purpose the harm of others, to bring them low and make them as vile as yourself—an impossible task you can never achieve, you nadir of abomination!

MARA: Mind your…

ANOUSHKA: You blame your nature for what you freely choose, in your spite, in your weakness. Bare no fangs at me, foul Ethiope! What will you do, kill me? Drink down my heart? You have soiled me already, dirtied me to the utmost, and anything else you can offer me is only release from torment!

MARA: Then we are both thirsting for an end to you! Bare your throat and let us be done with it!

LISETTE: Vlad, stop them!

VLAD: Mara, Anoushka, cease this chattering! One more threat, one more taunt, and I shall cry 'be damned' to both and cast you out together! Anoushka, you hope for a release from your curse, and I will work with you toward it! Mara, you too desire to exceed your present state? You would learn the deeper Coils that have cleansed my fear of fire? Then by all hell and heaven, you will respect Anoushka for her role in their creation!

LISETTE: Why teach her anything? What has she done to deserve the powers you command?

MARA: Let Anoushka answer that. The follower of virtue. Are the Coils truly a means to step from under God's curse? To be redeemed, forgiven, purified? If so, what manner of creature would withhold them from any supplicant? You, Anoushka, genius of these liberating magics: Are they not meant for all of us afflicted?

ANOUSHKA: They are meant to make you human once more! To free those who deserve it! I will not stand by and see my work abused to make a monster more monstrous—to erode the few checks that remain on your hostility and vice!

LISETTE: Do we really want to be human?

VLAD: What do you mean, my sweet?

LISETTE: I mean that as one of the *strigoi* I am exempt from injury, I won't crumple up into age and feebleness, I won't die of plague, I'm not at the mercy of any heathen with a saber and a cannon. Should I go back? Suffer childbirth? Marry and be the meek wife of some ham-handed man? I've seen wider vistas, deeper truth. I would not retreat from them even if I could.

ANOUSHKA: You speak with neophyte hubris. The urges, the violence…

LISETTE: What are they to me? So I live by the harm of others. Who does not? The prince taxes his subjects, the church takes tithes from believers, the soldier takes bread from the peasant, the pig and the chicken die for all. Every man is a thief, every child and woman too. We just know what we are.

MARA: Well spoken. We admit to ourselves what is at the bottom of our plates, and Anoushka? Tell me true if you have kept to your scruples, have refrained from the harm of those innocent mortals...

VLAD: She is not on trial here...

ANOUSHKA: No, I'll answer. Have I fed on human blood? Yes. Taken dark delight in it? Yes, indeed. But innocent? Oh, those men were so far from innocence that they could almost see your level, Mara...

MARA: That's good, it is well, it is begun! Start by judging! Start with the vicious and those who deserve it! You will end, oh mark my words, by seeing desert in all.

VLAD: Enough! I had called you here to discuss the question of Mara's disciples, but I find a larger question before us. What is the purpose of the Coils? No, stay your lips! Ponder. Contemplate. Do not speak with rash fire, but prepare your arguments well, calculate their merits, present them with peaceable dignity. I find myself needing refreshment. When I return, we will make our separate arguments.

(There followed a pause.)

MARA: If I may? The purpose of the Coils is to free us of your God-imposed limitations. That is all that they do. This raises the question: Why are we to be freed? What purpose does this emancipation serve? Why do we desire liberation?

We are despised by God and if He is all good, ought we not accept our punishment meekly? Yet none of us here would do so. I say that this is not because we are perverse by nature, but because our very situation is unjust. Why should one man who does evil—a slaver, a thief or a tyrant—live in comfort and luxury? At the same time, children and women who do no great wrong nor have the power to do so, they suffer at the hands of these evil men, often their very misery supports or is the entire substance of the oppressor's delight.

Anoushka, you were made a *ghul* against your will and you call it injustice, but did I will my slavery? Did Vlad will his captivity? Did any man dead of plague will it so?

The world is unjust and cruel, our curse is unjust and cruel, and to excoriate me as unjust and cruel is merely to complain that a fish in the water is wet, or that a stone flung in mud has let itself be dirtied.

All we are, all we can be, is what we make of ourselves. The Coils are a means to take freedom and power—no more than that, but that is no small thing. Like any power, be it wealth or position or strength of arms, it should be used for the betterment of those who possess it. If this means teaching it to others at cost, so be it. If it means using it upon enemies for advantage, so be that.

ANOUSHKA: These arguments are those of the victim who craves license to torment others. All this logic yields is a world full of torturers, each trying to worsen the lot of others that his own might not be lowest. It is short sighted. It is sad. In the end, conflict of all on all leads only and inexorably to greater suffering all around.

What if, instead of lording the Coils over our fellows, we use their power to improve the lot of each of us? Not only the *strigoi*, not only those who follow loyally some banner of the Dragon, but all who dare dream of kindness? Would not everyone benefit? By the Coils, the urge to rampage is reduced, which is a blessing both to us and to those around us. By the Coils, our need for blood, be it human or animal, is abridged. Surely that eases our predicament, even as it lessens the strain and abuse of the mortals we need.

The Coils are the art of overcoming not only our weaknesses, but our indwelling evil. To say they are merely power wrested unjustly from an unjust God in an unjust world is to look with the eyes of a child. Their power emerges when we make peace with our punishment, accept it, and acknowledge our responsibility to mitigate it. The Coils should be taught to those who would reduce the *strigoi* scourge upon the world—not solely because it is good that we do so, but because only such penitent creatures can truly wit their meaning.

WILLIAMS

VLAD: Lisette?

LISETTE: I think both of you are being foolish.

VLAD: Mara, Anoushka, please remain calm.

LISETTE: Anyone who thinks he knows what God is doing or planning is a fool. Anyone who thinks he can outwit the divine plan, or even comprehend it, is a spitting, screaming child. I was raised by men who were absolutely certain that they knew everything God wanted or had done, and there was no place in their beliefs for creatures such as we are, let alone the Coils that allow us to be otherwise. Let us not, then, enlist God into our plans, either as ally or enemy.

Our goal should be to find what is best for us, and let others take care of themselves. In this, I agree with Mara. Yet at the same time, to do evil as a joyless obligation is absurd. When you harm others for no reason you are, ultimately, permitting some vague notion of God to control your actions as much as if you help and protect others for no reason.

I do not know what we should do with the Coils or with ourselves, but I feel with every fiber that discussions of God are irrelevant to the question.

VLAD: Ha? Who is the witless kitten now, Mara? Who the vapid adornment, Anoushka?

Lisette is right. God is irrelevant to us. I see that now, but not because I have resigned myself to being naught but beast or demon. I am not human, and the Savior of mankind is not mine, nor are the rules and laws of humanity fit for a thing of my type.

Mara is right to say that hating ourselves for preying is contemptible. To pine for different circumstances, impossible ones, is to deny our right and our need to deal with what we are, and what we face. Yet Anoushka is wise to say that hating our prey for what we must do to them is also foolhardy. To fall before us is no virtue, no punishment, no sign of God's favor or wrath. It is simply the way of things.

Our difference is that we may make of ourselves what we wish, through the freeing power of the Coils. To try and make ourselves angels is doomed to fail, and to make ourselves devils is to waste our better potential. We have emerged from the weakness and strength of human lives to become something entirely else. The challenge now is not to despise what we are or revel in it, but to emerge yet again. We are ageless, timeless, deathless… what wonders might we achieve with further transfiguration?

Individually, you three had nothing but contention and spite for each other, but you have shown me a new path that you yourselves could not perceive. You deserve the light of my reflected illumination, for even in your ignorance you were its sparks.

This, then, is what we shall do. We shall teach the Coils to all who deserve their knowledge, but the way is to be straight and charged with peril. We shall know the worthy thus.

FIRST, that the student has no loyalty above his studies. His sole and ultimate duty is to seek the perfection of himself through the Coils, regardless of what his perfected nature is revealed to be.

SECOND, the student must recognize the mutability of all things. If he does not trust change, he can never use the Coils to overcome the curse of stagnation. The power of change, fortune and even base fickle randomness in this fallen world must be understood, acknowledged and embraced, even as we stand against it by our immobile inclining.

THIRD, the student must take responsibility for the path he walks, the changes he makes, the self he makes anew. We who are beyond Death cannot blame fear for our failings. We who are exempt from Age have no excuse for rash acts or foolish passions. We who possess unbounded Time have the chance to understand more fully, deeply and broadly than any mortal can. To ignore that opportunity is worse than murdering ten thousand souls, for it means murdering your own fullest future.

These are the circumstances under which my wisdom can flourish. What say you? Are they acceptable?

ANOUSHKA: One path cannot hold travelers to Hell and pilgrims on the path of salvation. There is no place for me that holds compromise with her.

MARA: As for me, I can stomach no lies that would whiten our crimson path. Blood leads us down. What truth can arise from self-swallowed and willful lies?

LISETTE: I will follow where my lord and lover leads me, but the grouping that rouses my passions is a pair, and not a multitude. What care I for grand conspiracies? Leave them, Vladislaus. Let them chew and worry upon each other while we delight in the raptures of desire. Leave wars against God, or for Him, to those who cannot merit love.

• • •

As the sun came up, I went to my discontented repose. Musing on my newfound appreciation for certain jests I'd heard among the polygamous Turks during my captivity, I fell into slumber.

More, I fell into dream—but a dream that had no sickly patina of nightmare, nor cloudy haze of half hopes. It was not a dream as men dream, nor was it the usual voiceless beast rumblings of *ghul* rest. Nay, this was clear and valid, a revelation with profound impact, rivaled only by that vision I had when I was made anew as one of the *strigoi*.

This, though, was no vista of crystal illumination. I found myself on a barren plain, with a veritable forest of the impaled surrounding me, stretching out in every direction. I saw my father and brothers, my Turkish captors, my Hungarian allies and Saxon foes. I saw my mortal wife and sons, dead all, and more, the many *ghuls* I have known, Fouchard and Anoushka and the walking dead of Paris and Jerusalem, even sweet Lisette, all immobilized by the wooden blow.

Surrounding me impaled was every person I had known, in my life or after.

Then a great rumbling shook the desolate soil, and it cracked open in a surge of heat and hungry red light. From below surged a monstrous serpent, the wings of a bat spread like sails from his scaly back, glassy eyes the size of wagon wheels, unblinking. Nostrils smoked like fresh-fired cannon as his mouth gaped wide, ringed with fangs as long as my arm.

It spoke as deafening thunder, each word accompanied by sulfurous smoke.

IMPALER, WHAT BRING YOU TO THE WORLD?

"Bring to the world? All that I owe it, which is nothing. Lest you ask, I take from it all I need, yea, and all else I desire."

YOU ARE BLIND. YOU BRING THE WORLD A PLAGUE OF MADNESS, A FLOOD OF EVIL VISIBLE IN THE FIRST TWO DROPS OF THREE. YET YOU SEE IT NOT, ENTRANCED BY WHAT YOU WISH AND OVER-LOOKING WHAT YOU SHOULD KNOW.

"Who are you, who dares insult me?"

Its laughter was deafening.

I AM YOU, IMPALER. I AM WHAT YOU COULD BECOME. IN THE FULLNESS OF TIME, YOUR FU-TURE SELF COULD BE THIS CREATURE OF FIRE AND HUNGER YOU BEHOLD.

"I don't believe you."

NOT EVEN IF I SPEAK THE FEAR YOU HIDE IN YOUR MOST SECRET HEART? THE FEAR THAT MARA IS DEGRADING, NIGHT BY PAINFUL NIGHT, INTO AN ARTLESS MONSTER UNWORTHY OF YOUR LINEAGE? THAT YOU ALREADY SEE, IN ANOUSKHA'S PARIS WRATH, THE SAME DECLINE? THAT LISETTE'S DECAY, THOUGH INEVITABLE, IS INVISIBLE ONLY BY VIRTUE OF HER NEWNESS TO DEATH?

That indeed gave me pause, for it had spoken a truth I had not durst think.

"How come you to speak to me thus?"

IN THE SLUMBER OF THE DEAD, TIME IS AS NOTHING. YOU HAVE A CHOICE TO MAKE, PRINCE OF THE NIGHT. A THREEFOLD PATH FORKS BEFORE YOU, WITH YOUR FOOT POISED TO TREAD IT. BE-HOLD, THAT WHICH YOU MAY ONE DAY FIND, IF THIS COMING NIGHT YOU SET YOUR COURSE ARIGHT.

In an instant, I found myself in a strange and glorious fortress. Towering walls surrounded me, and I stood among tall people, garishly dressed. They parted to make way for me, and as I strode forward I saw that I cast six shadows. Each shade was clear and sharp, with no candle flicker. I moved through light, but not wan and silver moon glow. Each object showed its bright, full colors.

The crowd began to chant my name, flinging gems and blossoms before me. I walked forward into the sun and was consumed.

102

Next, I found myself in more familiar darkness—the dark of a cloudy night, the only illumination red flickers in the distance. I scented smoke on the wind and instinctively fled it. I wore the wolf's shape by nature and could no longer recall the sensations of discourse and laughter and walking upright.

I scented man-flesh and, hungry, prowled. Three mortals, carrying spears of strange manufacture, sat in a clearing. They had no fire. I lunged forward to strike, and then they turned on me with too-wide grins.

"Far too easy," said the leanest one as his weapon pierced my breast. "Surely this cannot be Dracula."

In the third vision, I was in a crowd of *strigoi* and we were all mad with hunger. We struck each other, biting and clawing, drinking and spending ferociously that we might drink further before we were, ourselves, drained. I was in a red haze of fury punctuated by flashes of love, the intense lie of love that comes from drinking our false seducer blood. I choked back the love, killed through it. It seemed to take hours, days to fight them all, murder them all, consume soul upon soul. When they were dust I saw that I was in a dense maze of narrow streets, walls impossibly tall. I took the shape of a bat and flew up, weaving through the air only to see that everyone as corrupted, everyone was a *ghul*, we were all entangled at war and no mortals survived to feed us.

In the darkness, I awoke.

What can these visions mean?

Clearly I am in danger. My future is in danger. I am at risk of dying as a beast, at the tips of spears held by the contemptuous living. At the same time, the world is imperiled by a *ghul* plague, an overwhelming of the mortals by we who have surpassed them.

Less distant is the future I foresee, not with some faculty of the occult, but by dint of reason. Mara, the eldest of my blood, is not as she was. She has a beast's heart and her body begins to conform to it. I had hoped that Anoushka's uncharacteristic lapse in Paris was simply the cruelty of all our kind, but by the dragon's words I fear it a worse viciousness, one unique to mine.

This latter thought is particularly grim in light of the direction suggested by Anoushka's recent work. Easing those bonds which stay us from making more of our breed is clearly an undertaking fraught with far-reaching consequences. What irony, if the very woman who opens the gates to a multitude of our kind is doomed to breed only monsters!

Yet that first vision—my greatness recognized as I walk, feted, by pure light and into that light... what can that mean, if not the goal I seek? If not further transformation into something as different from *ghul* as *ghul* is from man?

The multitude cried out for me. I cannot deny my duty to them.

• • •

My father was honored by induction into the Order of the Dragon, and as his son I was a member as well. We were a sworn brotherhood, declared to the Turk's downfall and the triumph of Christianity, but we were not a military order like the Templars, nor a religious one like the Benedictines. My father's Ordo Dracul was a political order, subtle and discerning, admitting only men of good birth, high station and great potential. I still treasure the ring and the cup he won at that tournament which marked their inception, but their greatness was not strength of arms. It was their ability to move men and nations.

By the day of my death, the Order of the Dragon was a mockery of what it once had been, its members embattled with each other and more interested in prying power away from their Christian colleagues than from the Ottoman invaders.

Now, in the darkness, the Order is reborn. Is it not meet that the son of the dragon should, in turn, give birth to others?

The laws for the Coils are a start, but it is not enough to enjoy our esoteric advantages and hope that worthy students will, in time, seek us out. I have been shown that if my work does not grow and conquer, it will die out—or worse, be perverted into the tools of disaster.

Mara's loyalty lies on a knife-edge. She fears and covets my power, and I believe she loves and honors me as well as she is able. But the madness gnaws at her, and her followers threaten me and mine like the sword of Damocles.

Anoushka's infatuation with me died in Paris, alongside her hopes of what she might still be. What remains is a respect for my goals and abilities, but that is cold indeed next to passion. What heat remains within her is the white fear that madness and evil will overtake her... and perhaps a red glow of envy toward Lisette?

Ah, Lisette, my best hope, my shield and portion against despair. Will you turn in my hand, becoming surrender's advocate? It is only my due, having betrayed you, all unknowing to the bestial curse that treads first on Mara, holds Anoushka in the shadow of its heel, and sets its path to you?

Upon the fall of night, I came at once to Mara and spoke stern words to her—words I knew would be sweet to her harsh and wicked heart. I told her I would not stand to be dictated to nor threatened, that I would take my knowledge down to Hell before submitting to a woman's demands.

"You need me," she said, and her voice was near to a growl. "You have locked yourself in towers of thought while the business of blood and claw has dominated the streets below you. But if you would be more than a hermit in a moldering castle, you need force of arms. I can win force with force and make you a mighty lord again, even if your heart is that of a... scholar."

"I do not deny you your place," I told her. "You, my first-born and most perfect of monsters. But while you trumpet your strengths, admit your limits as well. Can you understand the Coils, or merely learn them?"

She lowered her head and I knew then I had her.

"The howls inside," she whispered. "Your wisdom is the only medicine that can quiet them." Then she looked up and her animal eyes were all envious hate. "You don't have them. You don't know what they're like! I know. You, you hear only their whispers and squeaks, not the full-throated roar like a lion. You are spared the curse you gave me."

"Be strong," I told her. "But temper your strength with submission. Only with your help, can I give you the cure you crave."

She nodded then, and for the first time since I saw her in the slaver's market, I saw her bow in defeat. It made me sad, in some part, although it is a great triumph. Breaking her to heel was needed, though I take no joy in this victory.

"What of Anoushka?" she asked. "She will not share her bounty with me but oh my Lord, I will not be her maid nor abase myself before her!"

"If you are content to walk with her, she shall be content to walk with you. Do you believe her way is false?"

"You know that I do."

"Then content yourself with our pledge to truth. In time, all falsehood will shrivel in the fires of our knowledge."

Anoushka I found in the forest, where she had called herself an unsuspecting feast—rabbits and squirrels blinked at unaccustomed night before she fell upon them.

I moved away unseen and found her again, when she had cleansed her lips in a stream.

"Anoushka," I greeted her. "We must speak."

"There is nothing to discuss."

"Not even bringing Mara to heel?"

She looked up at that. "You cannot train a serpent to harness," she said, but her voice betrayed the hope in her heart.

"Mara is no serpent. No, nor is she human. But she possesses Reason, and to that faculty I have made appeal. Do not roll your eyes! It is not Mara's first or favored tool, but she will make a try of thought when all else has failed."

"By what deft syllogism have you snared her, oh great philosopher?"

"Simply this: We have what she needs."

"The Coils."

"Anoushka, you see how the curse weighs on her, how she is at the edge of being a monster. Some part of her fights that still, and though she has wronged you—wronged you most direly!—you must surely wish to see the strength within her strike down the iniquity."

"Even if, as you say, her humanity is at war with her evil core I confess it: I would see them both dead, dust and damned."

"Can you not hope for her as you hoped for me? Have you cast aside all thought of renouncing our curse, of finding again the endless forgiveness of God?"

"It is so hard," she whispered. "The light within me dims nightly."

"Then take hope! The Coils have kept that wan fire lit, and in time may breathe it back to brilliance! Anoushka, you are the best hope of our kind! Yes, you have stumbled and have fallen, but when you rise you are still the swiftest mind among us! Married to your faith, there is no limit to what you can accomplish. Or would you give up, let Mara win by default, and confess that you are naught but evil?"

"I believe that she is naught but evil, and I would not give my gifts to her."

"So? Then deny her."

That gave her pause.

"What say you, my lord?"

"Deny her your gifts. Find the answer you seek, the solace you crave, transform yourself into a higher being◻ and do it before Mara's envious eyes. Do not argue your case with her, prove it, live it, yes, live again! Who could ask for a better revenge than to fling off the curse she gave you and leave her writhing within it?"

Slowly, she smiled.

"Your genius, lord Dracula, is your ability to turn the bitterest problems into solutions."

"I have faith in you, Anoushka, even if you doubt yourself. I think your path of light is the true one, and that at its end you will have the strength to forgive even her. But whether you would have her be the pinnacle of your grace, or crush her beneath your scorn, you will need her close, and you will need to seek. She can protect you, protect us all, as we find the answers all of us want. But in the end, she cannot force your knowledge from you. What say you?"

"It seems that forgiveness and revenge walk the same path. If they can travel in peace, so can Mara and I... at least until the road divides."

"That is all I ask."

WILLIAMS

I spent the remainder of the time until dawn strengthening my position with both the disputants and, when I felt my presence was beginning to wear upon them, planting seeds of thought and support among Lisette and even Mara's brood.

The next night's discussion was held with less heat and was therefore far more illuminating.

We all agreed that only a strict and solid hierarchy could contain creatures of our ilk, and to endure this hierarchy, needs must play to the strengths of its leaders. To this end, a three-fold rulership was devised, such that any crisis would be addressed by one with the skills to counter it. This tripartite structure would take the form of a triad of orders, each based upon dire and sober oaths, like a band of chivalrous knights. Together these three elite orders would guide and rule the larger Order of the Dragon, into which admission would be open to all *strigoi*.

The ultimate authority is, of course, myself.

Directly beneath me, as Boyars to a Prince, are the ranking members of those three oath-bound bands. To each is given a task, a sphere in which their word is supreme, and within that domain they can only be gainsaid by another of the same oath, whose rank is higher by virtue of deeper learning.

For the resolution of conflict between members who are both oath-sworn, but in which neither has a clear right of domain, that member with the greater knowledge of Coils takes precedence.

The oath-sworn shall have authority over all who have not pledged.

When two who are unsworn disagree, the superior place shall go to him who has made greater study of the Coils. Lowest of all are those who have asked membership in the Order, but who have yet to master even a single Coil.

The titles by which our number shall be known are as follows: He who has learned no Coils shall be called Slave; he with one Coil is Supplicant; he with two Coils is Scribe; he with three is Scholar; he with four is Initiate; and he with five is Adept. Any student who masters all six Coils shall be known by the title of Master.

If, in fullness of time, we progress on our great work and discover further Coils, additional titles shall be awarded. He who masters seven Coils is to be deemed Philosopher; he with eight Illuminus; and he with nine Coils at his command shall be called Architect.

Those titles are to be elaborated on formal occasions with descriptions. One who has greatest mastery of the Coils of Blood shall be entitled "of Hunger"; one who has most studied the Banes shall be entitled "of the Curse"; one whose deepest knowledge is of the Beast shall be entitled "of Terror"; one who has studied all Coils equally shall be entitled "of Equilibrium".

If even finer heraldry is desired, titles may be decorated to indicate secondary areas of study. Those who have partial knowledge of the Blood Coils may lengthen their title with "Sanguine" or "Bloody"; those with partial knowledge of the Bane Coils may append "Burning" or "Fiery" to their title; and those who have partial knowledge of the Beast Coils may elaborate their title with "Wild" or "Untamed".

The proudest commendations to title, however, are to be claims of honored oaths. The three oaths are as follows.

The first and most honored are to be the
Sworn of the Axe, with Mara my honored
daughter the first of their number. Their duty
is the protection of the Order, the defense of its
members, but above all the defense of our secrets. The prostitution of the Coils to those unworthy of them is a vile thought and one de-
serving of most severe punishment. Any who
teach the Coils to the unfit are to be bound by
the passion of the blood, twice tasted for each
secret divulged. He who wrongfully discloses
one Coil is to drink two times from his own
teacher, or his teacher's teacher if he himself
learned illicitly. If two Coils are taught, two
generations within the Order may bind his
heart. If three are taught, he shall know the
conflict of triple devotion.

Any who refuse this bondage may volunteer to
be impaled and left for the judgment of the sun.

In the tumult of battle and the chaos of peril, the Sworn of the Axe are supreme and their orders are to be obeyed without debate or hesitation. Let any who balk at their word in such circumstances be slain on the spot or bound for judgment.

While those who defy the Axe are to suffer, those who merit admission to it should rejoice. To them, let honor redound. As they shall be first to face peril for the Order, let the Order give them first pick of victims, lands and the rewards of honor.

This lauded task is not to be held lightly. Only those of the utmost martial prowess, who have already risked destruction to defend the Order, its members, its secrets or its properties, shall be eligible for this oath. Further, let none be shunned who is invited and refrains. To defend unto death is a high calling, and it is better to pass the cup of valor untasted than to poison that chalice with unclean lips.

115

Anoushka, the cross-breed chimera whose mind exceeds that of most men, shall take the first oath as the Sworn of the Dying Light, those who strive to deepen the three Coils we possess and explore further the fourth she has promised. By their arts we within the Order will push at the frontiers of our existence, learning to conquer our fear and wrath, our hunger and humility, our subjugation to the sun. She and hers will determine the course our unending studies should take, choosing those areas deemed fruitful.

Those who delve into the profound mysteries of our kind are to be respected, and their judgment weighted accordingly. In all disputes of authority, the Dying Light shall take precedence. They are to be our judges and councilors, even as the Sworn of the Axe are our soldiers and generals.

The Oath of the Dying Light is to be held out only to those who have gained for us some treasure of the occult previously unheld, be it secret knowledge stolen, arcane secrets discovered, or places of power seized and defended.

If the need should arise, the Sworn of the Dying Light shall judge any studies accused of being anathema to the Order or its goals. Already, I state here and for all time that THE PURSUIT OF ARTS WHICH SUBJUGATE THE STUDENT TO ANGELS, DEMONS, GHOSTS, OR ANY SPIRIT OTHER THAN THAT OF HIS OWN INDWELLING WILL, ARE FORBIDDEN AND DISGRACEFUL. Any follower of the Dragon who is caught in such self-abnegating idolatry is to be punished by that most final of fates: Death by drinking, and that his very soul be fed unto some worthy fellow student, that he might grow by the strength of it.

Shudder not at this punishment. Though the devouring of fellow *strigoi* is degrading and a sin, it is better that a sold soul be stolen for the Order than be a toy for demons below or an adornment for angels beyond.

Finally, my beloved Lisette is the first to be Sworn of the Mysteries. While the Dying Light is the center of our great work, and the Axe defends our very existence, the Mysteries are to give meaning to the course we take and the decisions we make. Each brother of the Order is to decide for himself who he is and must be, but the Order is greater than any single member. It is the duty of the Sworn of the Mysteries to take the view of centuries, making decisions for the Order as a whole, though not for any member within it. Their duty is to choose our destiny. In matters of collective action and decision, they have the authority to decide, and their writ is our law.

The Oath of the Mysteries is to be offered by acclamation. Only those who are vaunted by twenty of their fellows of the Dragon can be admitted, and only then if no single fellow, even the lowliest, speaks against their oath. Once sworn, the title to the Mysteries is permanent, regardless of action—save one.

Those who are sworn to the Mysteries are forbidden to taste the blood of the *strigoi* under any circumstances. Should they be fed on false love by force, it is meet that they seek their own destruction in fire or the sun. If they are too weak to escape their shame in that fashion, let them be cast down and shunned for their dishonor.

Worse, should they consume the blood and soul of a fellow *ghul*, they are to be punished by impalement and burning, at the hands of all who acclaimed them into their position.

Let the upholders of Mystery be pure, both in heart and in judgment.

WILLIAMS

These three divisions shall uphold the Ordo Dracul, as our three Coils set us apart from the lesser *strigoi* of the world. By these means, we shall spread our knowledge and will until it shades the world like the wings of the dragon.

So it is sworn. So it shall be.

By my hand, Vladislaus Dracul, Prince

of Wallachia, Master of Equilibrium

Credits
Written by: Greg Stolze
Vampire and the World of Darkness were created by Mark Rein•Hagen
Developer: Mike Lee
Editor: Ana Balka
Art Director: Pauline Benney
Layout & Typesetting: Colleen Denny
Interior Art: Daren Bader, Mike Chaney, Matt Hughes, Jeff Laubenstein, Raven J Mimura and Brad J Williams
Front Cover Art: Pauline Benney
Front & Back Cover Design: Colleen Denny

Author's Note
The historical Radu the Handsome only ruled Wallachia from the end of 1462 to 1473, when he was deposed by Basarab III Laiota. He died of syphilis in 1475. Liberties have been taken.

1554 LITTON DR.
STONE MOUNTIAN,
GA 30083
USA

WHITE WOLF
GAME STUDIO

© 2004 White Wolf Publishing, Inc. All rights reserved. Reproduction without the written permission of the publisher is expressly forbidden, except for the purposes of reviews, and for blank character sheets, which may be reproduced for personal use only. White Wolf, Vampire and World of Darkness are registered trademarks of White Wolf Publishing, Inc. All rights reserved. Vampire the Requiem, Werewolf the Forsaken, Mage the Awakening, Storytelling System and Rites of the Dragon are trademarks of White Wolf Publishing, Inc. All rights reserved. All characters, names, places and text herein are copyrighted by White Wolf Publishing, Inc.

The mention of or reference to any company or product in these pages is not a challenge to the trademark or copyright concerned.

This book uses the supernatural for settings, characters and themes. All mystical and supernatural elements are fiction and intended for entertainment purposes only. This book contains mature content. Reader discretion is advised.

For a free White Wolf catalog call 1-800-454-WOLF.

Check out White Wolf online at
http://www.white-wolf.com; alt.games.whitewolf and rec.games.frp.storyteller
PRINTED IN CANADA.